TOUCANS

by Golriz Golkar

Cody Koala

An Imprint of Pop!

popbooksonline.com

abdopublishing.com
Published by Pop!, a division of ABDO, PO Box 398166, Minneapolis, Minnesota 55439. Copyright © 2019 by POP, LLC. International copyrights reserved in all countries. No part of this book may be reproduced in any form without written permission from the publisher. Pop!™ is a trademark and logo of POP, LLC.

Printed in the United States of America, North Mankato, Minnesota

042018
092018

THIS BOOK CONTAINS RECYCLED MATERIALS

Cover Photo: Shutterstock Images
Interior Photos: Shutterstock Images, 1, 6, 9, 10, 15, 19, 20; iStockphoto, 5 (top), 5 (bottom left), 5 (bottom right); Art Wolfe/Science Source, 13; Ger Bosma/Alamy, 16; Pete Oxford/Minden Pictures/Newscom, 17

Editor: Meg Gaertner
Series Designer: Laura Mitchell

Library of Congress Control Number: 2017963423

Publisher's Cataloging-in-Publication Data
Names: Golkar, Golriz, author.
Title: Toucans / by Golriz Golkar.
Description: Minneapolis, Minnesota : Pop!, 2019. | Series: Rain forest animals | Includes online resources and index.
Identifiers: ISBN 9781532160295 (lib.bdg.) | ISBN 9781532161414 (ebook) |
Subjects: LCSH: Toucans--Juvenile literature. | Birds--Behavior--Tropics---Juvenile literature. | Rain forest animals--Juvenile literature. | Rain forest animals--Behavior--Juvenile literature.
Classification: DDC 591.739--dc23

Hello! My name is
Cody Koala

Pop open this book and you'll find QR codes like this one, loaded with information, so you can learn even more!

Scan this code* and others like it while you read, or visit the website below to make this book pop.

popbooksonline.com/toucans

*Scanning QR codes requires a web-enabled smart device with a QR code reader app and a camera.

Table of Contents

Chapter 1

Colorful Bird of the Rain Forest

Toucans are birds with large, colorful **bills**. Their bills help them scare away **predators** and find **mates**. Toucans also use their bills to grab food.

Watch a video here!

large, colorful bill

big, heavy wings

toes pointing in
two directions

Toucans have heavy wings, so flying takes a lot of work. Toucans often hop instead. Their toes point forwards and backwards. This helps them balance on branches.

Toucans can bark, growl, and croak like frogs.

Chapter 2

In the Flock

Toucans live in **flocks** of six to twelve birds. Every morning, they leave their nests to find food. They mostly stay in the treetops.

Learn more here!

Toucans are **omnivores**. They eat animals such as insects, lizards, and tree frogs. But they like fruit best. They swallow fruit whole and throw up the large seeds.

Toucans use their tongues to flick food down their throats.

Toucans sleep in small holes in trees. To fit, toucans bend their heads backwards. They tuck their bills under their wings. They look like balls of feathers!

Chapter 3

The Life of a Toucan

Every spring, mothers lay one to five eggs. After two or three weeks, babies hatch. Their eyes are closed. Their bills are small.

Learn more here!

After three weeks,
babies' eyes open and their
feathers grow.

After eight weeks, their bills are bigger and they leave their nests.

Toucans live up to 20 years.

Chapter 4

Coming Home

Toucans live in the rain forest in Mexico, Central America, and South America. They must stay safe from predators, such as jaguars, snakes, and large birds.

Complete an activity here!

Toucans are losing their **habitat**. People are cutting down trees where toucans live. But people can protect the rain forests and keep toucans safe.

Making Connections

Text-to-Self

Have you ever seen a toucan at the zoo? What did you think of it?

Text-to-Text

Have you read about other animals that live in the rain forests? How are they similar to and different from a toucan?

Text-to-World

Many animals are losing their homes because the forests are being cut down. Can you think of other reasons why people need to save trees?

Glossary

bill – a bird's beak.

flock – a group of animals of one kind (especially birds, sheep, or goats).

habitat – the place where an animal lives.

mate – an animal that is paired with another animal for having babies.

omnivore – an animal that eats both plants and other animals.

predator – an animal that hunts other animals.

Index

Online Resources

popbooksonline.com

Thanks for reading this Cody Koala book!

Scan this code* and others like it in this book, or visit the website below to make this book pop!

popbooksonline.com/toucans

*Scanning QR codes requires a web-enabled smart device with a QR code reader app and a camera.